Dedicated to my friend
Brother David Steindl-Rast,
the world's foremost teacher
of gratitude, on the occasion
of his 90th birthday.

The Little Book of Gratitude

Create a life of happiness and wellbeing by giving thanks

Dr Robert A Emmons, PhD

An Hachette UK Company
www.hachette.co.uk

First published in Great Britain in 2016 by Gaia Books,
a division of Octopus Publishing Group Ltd, Carmelite House
50 Victoria Embankment, London EC4Y 0DZ
www.octopusbooks.co.uk
www.octopusbooksusa.com
Text copyright © Robert A Emmons 2016
Design and layout copyright © Octopus Publishing Group Ltd 2016

Distributed in the US by Hachette Book Group USA, 1290 Avenue
of the Americas, 4th and 5th Floors, New York, NY 10104

Distributed in Canada by Canadian Manda Group, 664 Annette Street
Toronto, Ontario, Canada M6S 2C8

ISBN 978-1-85675-365-4

A CIP catalogue record for this book
is available from the British Library.

Printed and bound in China
10 9 8 7 6 5 4 3

Commissioning Editor Leanne Bryan
Art Director Juliette Norsworthy
Senior Editor Alex Stetter
Copy Editor Marion Paull
Designer Isabel de Cordova
Illustrator Abigail Read
Production Controller Sarah Kramer

Any information given in this
book is not intended to be
taken as a replacement for
medical advice. Any person
with a condition requiring
medical attention should
consult a qualified practitioner
or therapist. Only practice if
you feel able to. There should
never be pain.

Contents

Introduction

We are at the dawn of a global gratitude renaissance. Unprecedented interest in the science and practice of gratitude is so welcome because this is what gives us the strength of character to make life better not only for ourselves but also for others. A 2015 article in the popular journal *Scientific American* reported that, out of 24 strengths, including such powerhouses as love, hope, kindness, and creativity, the single best predictor of good relationships and emotional wellbeing was gratitude.

Gratitude is not just good medicine, though, a nice sentiment, a warm fuzzy feeling, or a strategy or tactic for being happier or healthier. It is also the truest approach to life. We did not create or fashion ourselves, and we did not get to where we are in life by ourselves. So living in gratitude is living in truth. It is the most accurate and honest approach to life.

What gives a movement its impetus, according
to gratitude teacher Brother David Steindl-Rast,
is not information, but enthusiasm and commitment.
The spark that can ignite a trend towards global
gratitude is the zeal of men and women who
discover that grateful living
makes life meaningful
and fulfilling. I invite
you to share in
my passion by
embracing and
contributing
to this global
gratitude
movement.

1
Unpacking Gratitude

Gratitude is, first and foremost,
a way of seeing that
alters our gaze.

Gratitude Matters

In schools, counselling clinics, health-care centres, workplaces, and even in the halls of academia, an increasing awareness that gratitude is vital for individual and collective flourishing is becoming more and more apparent.

Two main factors have driven this trend. First is the mounting evidence demonstrating that gratitude matters. Whether springing from the glad acceptance of another's thoughtfulness, appreciation of the splendour of nature, recognition of the good things in life, or from countless other magical moments, gratitude enhances nearly all spheres of our lives.

These effects are sustainable and quantifiable. Second, the practice of gratitude is readily accessible, available to everyone. You are never too old, too young, too rich, too poor, to live gratefully. We can produce gratitude in any season of life. This is part of its appeal. As we create gratitude, a positive ripple effect is generated through every area of our lives, potentially satisfying some of our deepest yearnings – our desire for happiness, our pursuit of better relationships, and our ceaseless quest for inner peace, health, wholeness, and contentment.

Yet the grateful state of mind, as accessible as it is, can be fleeting, difficult to sustain over the long haul unless practised with attention and intention. So we need to immerse ourselves in practices and techniques that will foster gratitude every day. This book contains science-based practices for growing your gratitude.

Living gratefully begins with affirming the good and recognizing its sources. It is the understanding that life owes me nothing and all the good I have is a gift, accompanied by an awareness that nothing can be taken for granted.

Gratitude is a way of seeing that alters our gaze

 ## ACTIVITY

Write It Down

In order to enter into this mode of thinking, let's begin with a simple exercise.

In the recent past, has there been a time when something good has come to you as a result of another person's action? Dwell on one experience in particular, and then write it down, following the model below. This exercise will be our starting point for examining what gratitude is and the various ways in which recognizing and affirming the good are the keys to unlocking fullness and freedom in our lives.

◇ The other day, I felt really glad when ....
(name or describe the person in your reflection)

◇ took the time, or made the effort to ....
(say what he or she did)

◇ I know that this person could have ....
(another path he or she could have taken,
perhaps in self-interest)

◇ but lucky for me, this person chose
to ....
(another brief description of what he or she did)

◇ This action ....
(say how it affected you, practically)

◇ and made me feel ....
(say how it affected you, personally)

◇ Thank you ....
(identify the person again)

What is Gratitude?

Grateful living is possible only when we realize
that other people and agents do things for us that
we cannot do for ourselves. Gratitude emerges
from two stages of information processing –
affirmation and recognition. We affirm the good
and credit others with bringing it about.

**In gratitude, we recognize that the
source of goodness is outside of ourselves**

Both elements in this definition count. Gratitude
involves a giver offering a gift to a receiver. We are
not grateful to ourselves but to another being. In
addition, in order for gratitude to exist, the giver
must act intentionally, typically at some self-sacrifice,
to bestow something worthwhile. The one receiving
the gift needs to recognize it as a gift, as something
good that was freely given. So gratitude engages
at least three different aspects of the mind. We
intellectually recognize the benefit, we willingly

acknowledge this benefit,
and we emotionally appreciate
both the gift and the giver.
The term "gift" is important
in this context because gifts
are unearned, things we are
not owed by the giver and
to which we are not entitled.

When we feel grateful, we
acknowledge that we have received a benefit and
recognize the value of it, and we appreciate the
intentions of the donor. We also recognize (perhaps
less consciously) that we didn't necessarily deserve
or merit the benefit. When we are grateful, we
recognize that we have no claim on the gift or
benefit received, and it was freely bestowed out of
compassion, generosity, or love. To recognize this
gift is the beginning of gratitude. Gratitude is not
simply a strategy or tactic for feeling better or for
increasing our personal happiness. It does something
much more than that. Gratitude enables a person
to feel good and also to do good.

Transformative Power

Stephen King, when asked by an interviewer on the US television programme *60 Minutes* why he chooses to write horror novels, peered through his thick glasses and retorted, "What makes you think I have a choice?" He literally could do no other than write books in this genre. Similarly, I feel that I can do no other than research and write about gratitude. I feel compelled to reach audiences with the message of the transformative power of this virtue.

Gratitude is the springboard for goodness and greatness

Believe it or not, my interest started as an assignment, which turned out to be the best I have ever been given. I was required to become the expert on scientific literature on gratitude for a conference. The problem was that there wasn't any! In the science of human emotions, gratitude was the forgotten factor. So I seized this opportunity and began conducting

research right away. I designed studies to measure the effects of gratitude, and canvassed theological, philosophical, and social science publications in an attempt to understand the essence of this universal strength. I soon came to believe that the capacity for gratitude is deeply woven into the fabric of the human species, and without gratitude it is impossible to flourish.

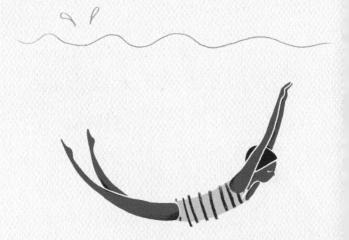

2
What Good is Gratitude?

The hand of gratitude
cannot be overplayed.

The Benefits of Gratitude

Numerous psychological, physical, and social benefits are associated with gratitude. A host of recent studies have examined its effects on health and wellbeing, and these clinical trials, laboratory experiments, and large-scale surveys have revealed that the practice of gratitude has dramatic, lasting, and positive results: every time.

 Keeping a gratitude diary for two weeks produced sustained reductions in perceived stress (28 per cent) and depression (16 per cent) in health-care practitioners.

 Gratitude is related to 23 per cent lower levels of stress hormones (cortisol).

 Dietary fat intake is reduced by as much as 25 per cent when people keep a gratitude journal.

 Writing a letter of gratitude reduced feelings of hopelessness in 88 per cent of suicidal inpatients and increased levels of optimism in 94 per cent of them.

◈ Gratitude is related to a 10 per cent improvement in sleep quality in patients with chronic pain (76 per cent of whom had insomnia) and 19 per cent lower depression levels.

Gratitude empowers us to take charge of our emotional lives and, as a consequence, our bodies reap the benefits. As a treatment, gratitude is cost effective, quick, and available to everyone. There are no known negative side effects. It is not a cure-all, of course, but it can significantly enhance the effects of conventional medical treatments.

The effects of gratitude are not limited to the physical realm. Just to give a glimpse into its benefits, gratitude increases self-esteem, enhances willpower, strengthens relationships, deepens spirituality, boosts creativity, and improves athletic and academic performance. Given the range of these positive outcomes, gratitude has fittingly been referred to as the quintessential positive trait, the amplifier of goodness in oneself, the world, and others, and as having unique ability to heal, energize, and change lives.

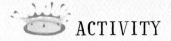 ACTIVITY

Count Blessings, Not Sheep

A number of studies have documented gratitude's beneficial effect on sleep quality. This exercise is designed to help you replace negative pre-sleep thoughts with thoughts that are more conducive to quietening the body and mind, so that getting to sleep is easier and overall sleep quality is improved.

◇ Over the next week, spend 15 minutes every evening writing about an event, experience, or relationship that you are grateful for. Writing it down rather than just thinking about it leads to a deeper level of processing, which has a longer, more sustained effect on your mood. About an hour before you go to bed is a good time to do this, and write about something different each night.

◇ After you get into bed, but before drifting off to sleep, try to focus on pleasant thoughts – good things happening to your family or friends; the

soothing sounds in your bedroom; how fortunate
you are to be in good health; future plans, such as
holidays or an upcoming trip; enjoyable things you
did during the past few days; how relaxed you are
feeling; good things that other people have done for
you in the past few days.

Your Brain on Gratitude

What brain structures and networks are activated when a person receives a gift and feels grateful? Gratitude is a complex state of interacting cognitive and emotional components, so it is likely that it involves multiple brain systems. It is no easy task to isolate these in the brain scanner. Nevertheless, recent neuroimaging studies offer important clues to what is going on inside the skull.

By measuring brain activity of participants, researchers found that gratitude, like other complex emotions, causes synchronized activation in multiple brain regions, involving social concepts, emotional responses, logic, and sensory processing. But gratitude also lights up parts of the brain's reward pathway and the hypothalamus, which controls the release of hormones that regulate bodily processes.

At the University of Southern California, researchers examined gratitude in the context of compelling stories of holocaust survivors receiving life-saving

help from others. Participants were asked to immerse themselves in the context of the holocaust, imagine how they would feel if they were in the same situation, and then rate how grateful they felt – all while the fMRI machine recorded their brain activity. Enhanced activity in areas of the brain besides the reward centre showed that gratitude activates centres involved in morality, connecting with others, and taking their perspective.

Gratitude is fertilizer for the mind, spreading connections and improving its function in nearly every realm of experience. Neuroscientist Rick Hanson has said that the brain takes the shape the mind rests upon. Rest your mind upon worry, sadness, annoyance, and irritability and it will begin to take the shape neurally of anxiety, depression, and anger. Ask your brain to give thanks and it will get better at finding things to be grateful for, and begin to take the shape of gratitude. Everything we do creates connections within networks of the brain, and the more you repeat something, the stronger those connection get. The mind can change the brain in lasting ways. In other words, what flows through the mind sculpts the brain.

What is the take-away message? The experience of gratitude really matters, not just for our moment-to-moment wellbeing, but also in the lasting residue woven into our very being.

 ## ACTIVITY

Brain with Gratitude

The need for novelty and change is hardwired into our brains. The substantia nigra/ventral segmental (SN/VTA), an area in the mid-brain, responds to novel stimuli. Whether you keep a diary, post gratitudes on your social media outlets, or just think grateful thoughts, focus on surprising events, unexpected kindnesses, new and unusual experiences and these will activate your SN/VTA. This area of the brain links memory and learning centres, so keeping your gratitudes fresh and new will be cognitively and neurally beneficial.

◇ An element of surprise helps us to hold on to gratitude. Try this exercise every other evening for a week. Ask yourself in what ways did my gratitude surprise me today? We can begin to seek out occasions to be surprised, and with that, use our mind to change our brain to benefit our mind.

◆ Travel can be a tonic for gratefulness. Is there somewhere that activates feelings of gratitude in you? Maybe a family getaway spot, a sacred spiritual site, or other place of natural beauty? In her book *The Sacred Depths of Nature*, biologist Ursula Goodenough wrote: "We are moved to awe and wonder at the grandeur... the richness of natural beauty; it fills us with joy and thanksgiving." The brain craves new, different, and unusual places. This need not be an exotic trip to a faraway land. Take a different route to or from work, go by bicycle instead of driving, explore your neighbourhood on foot. Your brain will thank you, your mind will be refreshed, and your creativity will soar.

Find your grateful place
and space

3
Why Gratitude Works

How can we explain
the phenomenal effects
of gratitude?

The ARC Model of Gratitude

Most people intuitively know when they should feel grateful, but often genuine gratitude remains a transient and unpredictable occurrence. Once we know why and how it works, real gratitude can become a regular response. What gratitude does is amplify, rescue, and connect. This is the ARC model.

1 Gratitude amplifies:

The good that we see in ourselves, in others, in the world, is multiplied and magnified through a grateful outlook. Gratitude locks in this goodness, sealing it deep into our being so it appreciates in value. The prolific and profound writer and philosopher G K Chesterton said, "I do not think there is anyone who takes quite such a fierce pleasure in things being themselves as I do. The startling wetness of water excites and intoxicates me: the fieriness of fire, the steeliness of steel, the unutterable muddiness of mud."

We've all heard of paranoia, but what about pronoia? This is the belief that others are conspiring to help us. "I suspect people of plotting to make me happy," as J D Salinger put it in his novella *Raise High the Roof Beam, Carpenters*. Grateful people are pronoids, expecting and seeing benevolence in the world, always aware of and easily sharing their gratitude, amplifying the good in themselves and in others.

Gratitude shines a light on goodness

2 Gratitude rescues: Left to their own devices, our minds tend to hijack each and every opportunity for happiness. Negativity, entitlement, resentfulness, forgetfulness, ungratefulness all clamour for our attention. Whether stemming from our own thoughts or the daily news headlines, we are exposed to a constant drip of negativity. Doom and gloom are on the horizon as financial fears, relational turmoil, global conflicts, and health challenges threaten us.

We are worn down by it, emotionally and physically exhausted. To offset this constant negativity, we need to create and take in positive experiences. Gratitude is our best weapon, an ally to counter these internal and external threats that rob us of sustainable joy. Gratitude rescues us from thieves that derail our opportunity for happiness, and gets us back on track to contentment and inner peace.

3 Gratitude connects: We cannot and do not live alone. Human relationships would unravel without gratitude. This is the moral cement, the all-purpose glue, the emotional filling that squeezes into the cracks between people, strengthening and solidifying these relationships. Without gratitude we'd be in relational ruin. Organizations, families, societies would crumble.

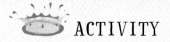 **ACTIVITY**

The Dos & Don'ts of Rescuing Yourself from Anxiety

◈ **Do switch your focus to other people**
By focusing on the benevolence of others, gratitude helps us feel more nourished by a supportive network. A grateful response to life keeps memories of cherished relationships and the kindnesses of others alive longer and means we are less likely to take them for granted.

◈ **Do focus on what you have received**
We can focus on what we have received or on what has been withheld. The "surplus" mode will increase our feelings of worth; the "deficit" mode will lead us to think how incomplete our life is.

◈ **Do acknowledge the emotions you feel**
Gratitude recruits other positive emotions, such as joy, contentment, and hope, and these produce direct physical benefits through the immune or endocrine systems. A grateful perspective on life is a stress-buster, so grateful people are more

equipped than others to deal with uncertainties, ambiguities, and situations that trigger anxiety.

 Do not compare yourself to others
If you compare yourself with those whom you perceive as having more advantages, you feel less secure. Wanting more is related to increased anxiety and unhappiness. A healthier comparison is to contemplate what life would be like without a pleasure that you now enjoy.

 Do not be envious or live a life of regret
Gratitude buffers you from emotions that drive anxiety. You cannot be grateful and envious, or grateful while harbouring regrets.

 Do not isolate yourself from others
The need for attachment and social contact lies deep within all of us. Although having time to ourselves is important, loneliness is a negative emotional state. We may choose to spend time alone but we don't choose to be lonely.

 # ACTIVITY

Reach Out and Touch Someone

Gratitude can trigger the need for physical contact just as touch can make us feel more grateful. Next time you are feeling grateful to someone, give him or her a hug, or a touch on the hand or shoulder.

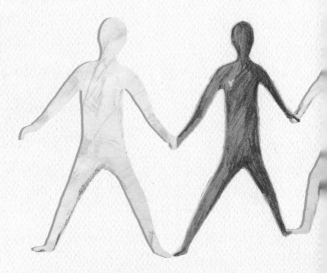

◇ Did your feelings of gratitude become stronger as a result?

◇ Did you feel a closer connection with the other person?

◇ How can you sustain that feeling over time?

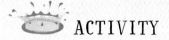 ACTIVITY

Gratitude to Those who Help a Loved One

An often overlooked opportunity for gratitude is when a friend or family member receives a blessing. Think of a time when a loved one was the recipient of a kindness performed by a mutual friend. Perhaps that person was available when you weren't, provided a service you weren't able to, or otherwise offered comfort and support to your loved one. What was the occasion and how did you show your thankfulness?

 ## ACTIVITY

Conduct an Audit

What have I received? What have I given?
How have I caused difficulty for others?
These questions form the basis of Naikan,
a meditative practice developed in Japan by
Yoshimoto Ishin, a devout Buddhist. Its purpose
is to help us feel the truth of our lives through
rigorous self-examination. Reflection upon these
questions promotes insight, a sense of indebtedness,
the emergence of gratitude, and a consequential
decision to shift from a focus on the self to a
deeper attentiveness and sensitivity towards others.
With this comes a keener appreciation of, and
gratefulness for, help and benefits received.

 Every day for a week, spend an hour
reflecting on those basic three questions
in relation to a different person in your life.

 Reflect on personal roadblocks that interfere
with your ability to express gratitude in your
closest relationships.

◇ Ask a close friend or family member to help you see your weaknesses and flaws. Be honest and try to receive whatever he or she says with humility.

◇ Set aside time for personal confession and self-examination. Ask yourself, who have I harmed by my thoughtlessness or self-centredness? Write an apology to make things right between you and that person. Naikan encourages us to examine both our past and our present in honesty and truth in terms of not only the support we have been given, but also the choices we have made to the detriment of others. As we become more conscious of the gift of our existence, our interdependency with others, and our responsibility for our actions, we experience a profound sense of appreciation and gratitude for our lives.

4

Making Your Mind Up

When you control your mind,
you control your world.

Celebrate the Goodness

Across the board, the grateful mind reaps a massive advantage. As we have seen, the results of rigorously conducted studies have given us a glimpse of what life can look like when a person is gripped by gratitude. However, to experience the sustainable benefits of practising gratitude, we must become habitually aware of gratitude-inspiring events and circumstances, then declare and share these with others. This is the key to an effective guided practice.

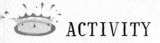 ## ACTIVITY

Three Good Things

Think about three things that went well
for you yesterday.

◇ Why did they go well?

◇ How grateful did they make
you feel?

◇ Did you tell anyone about them?

Sharing our victories, whether large or
small, helps us to celebrate the goodness
in our lives. Do this every day for the
next week.

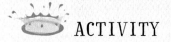 **ACTIVITY**

Gratitude Recounting

The road to living a life of gratefulness and appreciation is not simply a matter of repeating positive affirmations or conjuring up grateful feelings, but rather it is a way of perceiving the countless ways in which we are blessed and supported as we go about our daily lives. It is a daily discipline whereby you consciously and deliberately choose to focus upon all that is working in your life, the ordinary and the extraordinary.

◈ Keep a journal and, each day, write down up to five things that you are grateful or thankful for, and the source or provider of these good things. If you can't think of five things, note down as many as come to mind. Writing them down helps to cement your feelings of gratitude and you can then look back at your record of these gratitude-inspiring blessings.

Cultivate Gratitude

When we respond to our lives, our past as well as events in the present, from a point of view of gratitude and appreciation, the way we interpret our experiences begins to shift and soften as we begin to soften inside.

Consequently, we may notice that our behaviour begins to change as well. In other words, as the interpretation of my life broadens and shifts, so does my ability to respond to my life and to others differently. In fact, this capacity for existential resiliency and emotional flexibility in the face of an often disappointing reality is a hallmark of those who add the cultivation of gratitude and other positive qualities to their emotional repertoire.

In a Thanksgiving Day *Huffington Post* blog, actress Jamie Lee Curtis wrote: "This Thanksgiving I am mostly grateful for my own mind's ability to change my attitude and the message." There are several effective evidence-based strategies for training the mind to think gratefully. We can cultivate gratefulness by structuring our lives, our minds, and our words in such a way as to facilitate awareness of gratitude-inducing experiences.

Our minds are comparison-making machines. We make mental comparisons between the way things are and how things might have been different, or how things were, or how things might be in the future. Some forms of comparison thinking are deadly for our gratitude, such as when we envy those around us who appear to be better off than we are, and we think, "It could have been me." Other forms of comparison thinking give us a deeper appreciation of what we might otherwise fail to notice, or we might feel entitled to or take for granted. In gratitude, we say, "It could have been different."

Do a Downward Comparison

When we encounter misfortune along our journey, we can suddenly realize, by comparison, how blessed we are. Seeing others struggle with poverty or illness or discrimination helps us not to take our own abundance or health or privilege for granted.

 Can you recall a situation in which you encountered misfortune that, in turn, increased your awareness of your own blessings?

The Attitude of Gratitude

Our language reflects our thoughts, and our thoughts partially create our reality. Grateful people freely use words such as gifts, givers, blessings, blessed, fortune, fortunate, and abundance. Less grateful people are preoccupied with burdens, curses, deprivations, and complaints. The language of gratitude draws our attention to the positive contributions that others have made to our lives.

It is possible to shift self-defeating talk to an internal dialogue cloaked in thankfulness. Grateful people are masters at turning their minds to the ways in which they're supported and sustained. Once you start to notice kindness, more good actually begins to come your way.

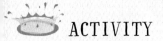 **ACTIVITY**

What If?

This technique involves focusing on the surprisingly good things in your life that might never have happened. It's just a different method of focusing attention, and is a very powerful way to create gratitude. We are constantly examining how our lives are going right now based on how things might have been, how poorly things were going in the past, how things might be in the future, how people around us are doing. Sometimes these comparisons are detrimental to our wellbeing but sometimes they are just the opposite. The trick is to use them in a way that makes them beneficial.

 Imagine what your life would have been like if you had not taken a certain life-changing path, such as moved house, or left your job to pursue a new opportunity.

 Try doing this two or three days in a row, each time bringing to mind something else about your life that might have turned out differently.

Grateful Reflection

One highly effective technique for training the mind to think gratefully has been dubbed the George Bailey effect, after the central character in the film classic *It's a Wonderful Life*. On the brink of taking his own life, Bailey is shown what the world would have been like had he never been born. This exercise forces George to realize just how rare and precious the good things in his life actually are, which instantly cures his depression.

In one study of the George Bailey effect, couples wrote about ways in which their lives would have been different if they had never met their spouse. This exercise had a greater impact on their happiness than when they reflected on what they really appreciated about their husband or wife!

5

Gratitude Myths

Does gratitude make us lazy? Naive?
Debunking common myths
and misconceptions.

The Case for Gratitude

Even armed with years of scientific data, making the case for gratitude can still be an uphill battle. Objections to and reservations about gratitude include protests that we should not devote a lot of energy to cultivating that specific attitude.

While I appreciate the questions and concerns people have about gratitude, I think many of the objections are based on fundamental myths or misconceptions about what gratitude really is. Unfortunately, these misconceptions deter people from practising gratitude and so reaping its many rewards. Here's my take on five of the most pervasive myths about gratitude.

Myth 1:
Gratitude Leads to Complacency

I've often heard the claim that if you're grateful, you're not going to be motivated to challenge the status quo or improve your lot in life.

You'll just be satisfied, lazy, and lethargic, perhaps passively resigned to an injustice or to a bad situation. In fact, studies suggest the opposite is true – gratitude drives a sense of purpose and a desire for change.

My colleagues and I have found that people are actually more successful at reaching their goals when they consciously practise gratitude. In one study, people identified six personal goals they intended to work on for ten weeks. These covered academic, spiritual, social, and health-related goals, such as losing weight or eating healthily. Participants randomly assigned to keep a gratitude journal, recording five things for which they were grateful once a week,

A grateful heart does not sit still

exerted more effort towards achieving those goals than participants who were not asked to practise gratitude. Not only that, the grateful group made 20 per cent more progress towards their goals, and continued to strive harder, than the non-grateful group.

Keeping a gratitude journal consistently results in feeling more energetic, alive, and alert. Other research has shown that gratitude inspires good-neighbourly behaviour – generosity, compassion, and charitable giving, none of which suggests passivity or resignation. Rather, it indicates that gratitude motivates people to go out and do things for others – to give back some of the goodness that they themselves have received.

For a study published in the journal *Motivation and Emotion* a few years ago, my colleagues and I found that kids who were more grateful than their peers at age ten were, by age fourteen, undertaking more community activities and were more socially integrated. These grateful youngsters didn't sit back and chill. They were out in the world, trying to make life better for others.

Myth 2:
Gratitude is Just a Naive Form of Positive Thinking

Some say that gratitude ignores the reality of pain, suffering, and adversity, both traumatic upheavals and the slow drip of everyday annoyances, but evidence shows that gratitude is much more than thinking pleasant thoughts.

In fact, gratitude can be very difficult because it requires that you recognize your dependence on others, and that does not always feel good. You have to humble yourself, in the sense that you have to become a good receiver of others' support and generosity. That can be very hard – most people are better givers than receivers.

Feelings of gratitude can sometimes stir up related feelings of indebtedness and obligation, which doesn't sound like positive thinking at all. If I am grateful for something you provided to me, I have to take care of it and use it in accordance with your wishes.

That's simply the decent thing to do. I might even have to reciprocate at some appropriate time in the future. That type of indebtedness or obligation can be perceived very negatively and it can cause us real discomfort.

The data bears this out. When people are grateful, they aren't necessarily free of negative emotions. They don't necessarily have less anxiety or less tension or less unhappiness. Practising gratitude magnifies positive feelings more than it reduces negative ones. If it was just positive thinking, or just a form of denial, you'd experience no negative thoughts or feelings when you're keeping a gratitude journal, for instance. But, in fact, people do.

So gratitude isn't just a nice warm feeling. It has responsibilities that go along with it that can make it difficult or challenging.

Myth 3:
Gratitude Makes Us Self-effacing

If I am grateful, does the credit I give to others come at my own expense?

Does it mean I fail to see my contribution to the good that has befallen me? The myth here is that when people recognize the ways in which others have helped them, they risk overlooking their own hard work or natural abilities.

Research suggests that this is simply not the case. In one study, researchers told participants that they could win money for doing well in a difficult test.

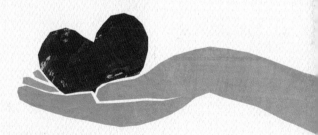

Then the participants were given a hint that would help them get a high score.

All participants regarded the hint as helpful but only those who felt personally responsible for their own score felt grateful for the hint. Gratitude was actually associated with a greater sense of personal control over success.

This has been corroborated in other studies. Grateful people give credit to others, but not at the expense of acknowledging their own responsibility for their success. They take credit, too. It's not either/or – either I did this all myself or somebody else did it for me. Instead, they recognize their own feats and abilities while also feeling gratitude towards the people – parents, teachers – who helped them along the way.

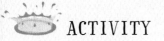

ACTIVITY

Celebrate a Victory

Recall an important personal success that you are grateful for, such as winning an award, achieving a victory on the athletics field, receiving an academic distinction, getting the job promotion. Maybe you had to overcome enormous obstacles, demonstrating determination and perseverance. The steeper the challenge, the sweeter the victory and the deeper the gratitude. Share it with others.

Myth 4:
Gratitude isn't Possible — or Appropriate — in the Midst of Adversity or Suffering

On the contrary, in these circumstances, gratitude is vital. When faced with adversity, gratitude helps us to see the big picture and not feel overwhelmed by current setbacks. It can actually motivate us to tackle the challenges before us.

It can be hard to take this grateful perspective, but research suggests it is possible, and worth it. Consider a study published in *The Journal of Positive Psychology*. Participants were asked to recall an unpleasant memory they still found upsetting. They were chosen randomly to complete one of three different writing exercises, one of which involved focusing on positive aspects of the upsetting experience and considering how it might now make them feel grateful. The gratitude group reported feeling more closure and less unhappiness than participants who didn't write about their experience from a grateful perspective. The grateful writers weren't told to deny or ignore the negative aspects of their memory, yet they seemed more resilient in the face of those troubles.

Similarly I once asked people suffering from severe neuromuscular disorders to keep a gratitude journal over two weeks. Given that much of their lives involved intense discomfort and visits to pain clinics, I wondered whether they'd be able to find anything to be grateful for. Not only did they find reasons to be grateful, but they also experienced significantly more positive emotions than a similar group who didn't keep a gratitude journal. The gratitude group also felt more optimistic about the upcoming week, more connected to others (even though many of them lived alone), and reported getting more sleep – an important indicator of overall health and wellbeing.

So again, this is a gratitude myth that can be debunked. Science verifies that we can cultivate or maintain an attitude of gratitude through hard times, and we'll be better for it.

ACTIVITY

Convert Adversity into Prosperity

Even when bad things happen, they ultimately have positive consequences, which we can then be grateful for. Try to focus on those outcomes.

◈ What kinds of things do you now feel thankful or grateful for?

◈ What personal strengths have grown out of your experience?

◈ How has the event made you better able to meet the challenges of the future?

◈ How has the bad experience benefited you?

◈ How has it put your life into perspective?

Myth 5:
You have to be Religious to be Grateful

This myth is easy to bust. The new science of gratitude has clearly shown that people can have a grateful disposition even if they're not religious.

Also, feeling grateful to God doesn't preclude feeling grateful to other potential sources of goodness. In some of my research, we asked people to identify the sources of their success and positive qualities, such as their intelligence or attractiveness. Those who scored high in gratitude were more likely to give credit to God, but they were also more likely to give credit to other people, genetics, and hard work as well.

Explore the Complexities

Many of these myths spring from a misconception that gratitude is a simplistic emotion. Part of what keeps me passionate about gratitude is that it is deceptively complicated. Once we appreciate these complexities, we are in a better position to enjoy the strengths and goodness gratitude can bring.

 ACTIVITY

Ask Yourself

 Have any of these myths held you back from fully embracing gratitude? Which ones?

Ⓓ What other myths did you once think were true? How did they fail to hold up to scrutiny?

Ⓓ A friend may say, "Yes, gratitude is a good idea, and people would be better off if they practised it. But not me. You don't know what I'm going through. Given my situation, gratitude is not realistic." How would you respond?

6
The 3 Stones of Gratitude

Build your gratitude
on a solid foundation.

Taking Steps Towards Gratitude

Three steps are necessary to find the kind of
gratitude that stokes joy over the long-term –
looking for, receiving, and giving back the good.
A powerful meditation to set you on the path is
to focus on these steps. If you carry three small
stones with you, these will be tangible reminders
of the three steps to gratitude.

1. Joy — Look for the Good

To feel gratitude we have to be attuned to the good in our lives, and this gives rise to joy, which is the pure and simple delight in being alive.

Joy is an intensification, strengthening, deepening, and elevation of the whole awareness of life. To have joy, our eyes must be wide open in gratitude.

> "Joy is where the whole being is pointed
> in one direction, and is something man never
> hoards but always wants to share."
>
> Frederick Buechner,
> author and theologian

We can easily rob ourselves of joy by seeing the good merely as effects of prior causes or as entitlements rather than gifts. In fact, joy is the linchpin between delight and adversity, and to find it we must look for

Gratitude is the
gateway to joy

the good in the bad. Joy is especially treasured after
a time when sorrow or grief has dominated our lives.
Grateful reflection teaches us that we need to
recognize the numerous ways in which the world
supports, nurtures, and sustains us.

Joy awakens all our senses, energizing mind and body.
Both gratitude and joy reflect a fully alive, alert, and
awake state of attunement between the self and the
world, which is necessary for sustainable wellbeing.

2. Grace — Receive the Good

Once we see the good, we must learn to accept it, and absorb it into the very nature of our being, which is challenging because most of us are not used to getting something for nothing and want to earn whatever comes our way.

Grace allows us to accept the good without crippling feelings of indebtedness, embarrassment, or a sense of inferiority. When we recognize that the gift or benefit has been freely bestowed out of compassion, generosity, or love, no matter whether we deserve it or not, we can feel the joy in receiving. Often we pay too much attention to the downside of receiving. Grace, by showcasing the goodness of the giver, helps us to keep our priorities straight.

 **ACTIVITY**

This is Amazing Grace

What does grace look like and feel like to you?
How would you describe it? Ask yourself the
following questions.

 Have you ever experienced grace? What were
the circumstances? What were the distinguishing
features of the grace you received?

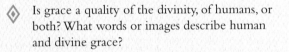 Is grace a quality of the divinity, of humans, or
both? What words or images describe human
and divine grace?

 Is grace a frequent or rare experience for you?
If rare, what has blocked you from receiving
grace in your life?

3. Love – Give Back the Good

Real gratitude promotes a desire to reflect the goodness received by creatively seeking opportunities for giving. This is love, the third dimension, or stone, of gratitude.

The motivation for giving back the good resides in the grateful appreciation that we have lived by the grace of others. Gratitude makes those who receive grace long to give it back. In giving back the good, gratitude becomes thanksgiving and the cycle between receiving and giving is completed.

> "There are two kinds of gratitude:
> the sudden kind we feel
> for what we take; the larger
> kind we feel for what we give."
>
> Edward Arlington Robinson,
> Pulitzer Prize-winning poet

 ACTIVITY

Share the Goodness

How can you show gratitude for the many gifts you have received? Resolve to give back one act of goodness each day for a week.

 Tell a friend about something someone did for you, and say why it mattered.

 Invite a friend to do something you know that he or she has always wanted to do but never had the opportunity.

◇ Offer to run an errand or perform a chore for a friend or neighbour, one you know they don't enjoy, such as raking leaves or mowing the lawn.

◇ When people serve you in a shop or restaurant, or anywhere else, let their supervisor know what an amazing job they are doing.

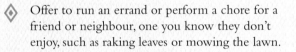

**We must never forget
that thanksgiving is a word of action**

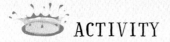 ACTIVITY

The Flow of Gifts

This simple exercise encourages you to consider the good things in your life and the ways in which that goodness can be passed on to others.

◇ Focus for a moment on your life's gifts. These could be simple, everyday pleasures, people in your life, your personal strengths or talents, moments of natural beauty, or gestures of kindness you have received from others. We might not usually think about these things as gifts but that is how I want you to think about them. Slowly repeat the word "gift" or a phrase such as "I am gifted" or "I have been gifted" several times.

◇ Now try to experience these gifts. Consider the effort or thoughtfulness of the giver of each one. Ponder how little you've done to earn or merit the gift, yet here it is anyway. Enrich the gift by savouring it, relishing it, delighting in it, thinking about what your life would be like without it. Instead of taking it for granted, take it as granted.

Bring to mind surprising or unexpected gifts that you have received.

◈ We are not the final destination in the flow of these gifts. Rather, we find ourselves mid-stream. Good things flow to us but they also flow from us to others. We are simultaneously receivers and givers. In some spiritual traditions, the term

"All goods look better
when they look like gifts."

G K Chesterton,
writer and philosopher

"favour" is used. Think about how you have received favour today, and how you can pass along that favour to others. Visualize a stream of water of remarkable clarity, with no beginning and no ending, flowing into you and then on from you.

As a channel for gifts and favour, ask yourself, "How can I pass along this goodness to those in need? How can I share these gifts with others?" Commit to not hoarding them. In what way can you give back for the many ways you have been gifted? What are some concrete ways in which you can honour the giver? Can you "pay it forward"? Who can you tell about this gift you received? Let your gratitude overflow into blessing, filling those around you.

7
Gratitude Metaphors

Gratitude is the emotional
putty of relationships
– it seals up the cracks.

Putting Gratitude in the Picture

Aristotle's oft-cited phrase, "the soul never thinks without a picture", is especially relevant as we contemplate communicating the power of gratitude. How we think about gratitude revolves around metaphor. Gratitude metaphors inspire and drive personal change, encouraging us to go deeper into grateful living. Lock and key metaphors are especially common. Gratitude has been referred to as "the key that opens all doors", that which "unlocks the fullness of life", and the "key to abundance, prosperity, and fulfillment."

As a professor and public speaker, I traffic in the language of metaphor for a living. I have seen how metaphors make ideas come alive, stirring the imagination, shaping thought and action. Metaphors are not simply words. They create meaning and understanding, stimulate and guide, and help us to see old truths from fresh perspectives.

"Gratitude is the Fabric of our Lives"

Humans have an innate longing to belong, and gratitude, or the lack of it, has its biggest impact in the domain of relationships.

It is the thread that stitches us together. Each act of gratitude contributes to the overall patchwork but these threads are frail. Ingratitude, forgetfulness, resentment, entitlement are forces that weaken and can ultimately unravel the fabric. However, it can be strengthened in some proven, effective ways that allow us to reap the rewards of grateful living.

Gratitude powers our every interaction

 **ACTIVITY**

Write a Gratitude Letter

Think about a person in your life whom you have never taken the time to thank properly. Is it a teacher, mentor, coach, close personal friend?

◇ Spend at least 30 minutes composing a letter of gratitude of around 250 words to this person. Describe specifically why you are grateful, how he or she has affected your life, and how often you reflect on his or her efforts.

◇ If you feel you can deliver the letter in person, arrange to visit but do not say what the visit is about. Read your letter out loud to the recipient. Be prepared to have your heart touched and to see the other person's heart touched as well. Allow yourself to open up to whatever the experience has in store for both of you, and spend some time talking about it with your friend.

"Gratitude is the Ultimate Performance -enhancing Substance"

Unlike other performance-enhancers, gratitude is always legal, has no side effects, and you cannot overdose on it. Gratitude improves performance in every domain of life that has been studied.

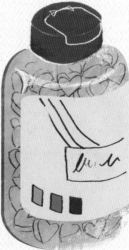

 ACTIVITY

Get Moving

Being active makes us grateful. Sometimes it is as simple as ensuring good posture. Bad posture makes us feel passive, dull, sleepy, and sluggish. Slumped shoulders produce slumped mood. Conversely, straightened shoulders make us feel determined, confident, enthusiastic, poised to take in the good.

 Right now, wherever you are, sit up straight.

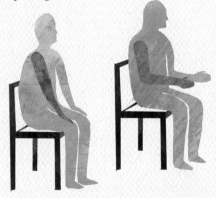

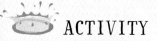 **ACTIVITY**

Body Naikan

The practice of Naikan was mentioned in
Chapter 3 (page 39) as a method for cultivating
gratitude. A reflective meditation on what
our bodies do for us can lead us into a greater
awareness of how we are sustained and supported
through our physical being.

Our senses act as a gateway to gratitude. Someone
said that gratitude is the sixth sense – it makes all the
other senses come alive. Through our ability to touch,
see, smell, taste, and hear, we appreciate what it means
to be human and what a miracle it is to be alive.

Take taste, for example. The average person has 10,000
taste buds, and they are replaced every two weeks or
so. Isn't that amazing? The olfactory receptors in your
nose are working in concert with our taste buds to
enable us to experience gastronomic bliss. How have
we repaid our teeth for functioning so well for us?
Have we taken care of them? A Naikan reflection of
ourselves like this can stimulate a deeper appreciation
of the miraculous creation that is the human body.

"Gratitude is the Universal Currency"

The language of gratitude is international. Thanksgiving customs, traditions, and rituals take place all over the world. Gratitude lets us see ourselves as part of a larger, intricate network of sustaining, reciprocal relationships. As the emotional force behind reciprocity, gratitude serves as a key link in the dynamic between receiving and giving.

"Gratitude is an Operating System, not an App"

Gratitude is not just an add-on, an afterthought, another item to be included on, and then crossed off, one's daily to-do list. It is a fundamental life orientation, an entirely new operating system. This is why apps for cultivating gratitude are rarely successful in creating sustainable changes. They provide a glimpse into the grateful life, but are insufficient to fill the job description.

"Gratitude is Gifted, not Scripted"

How often do we say thank you in a perfunctory way without putting our heart into it, merely to eliminate that nagging feeling of indebtedness? Whoever you are saying thank you to knows whether you really mean it or not, though, so try adding gratitude to your thanks. In a study conducted at the Wharton School of Business at the University of Pennsylvania, those who used the phrase "I am really grateful" in expressing thanks for a favour were seen as more genuinely thankful than those who simply wrote, "Thank you so much."

 **ACTIVITY**

Mindful Thank Yous

Practise mindful thank yous for the next seven days. When thanking someone who has done something for you, whether large or small, be specific, comment on the effort it has taken, and the cost, and keep the focus on that person. For example, "Thank you for bringing me my tea in bed. I really appreciate you getting up early each day. You're so thoughtful." The key to effectiveness is to achieve some separation between the kind act and your expression.

> **Gratefulness**
> **is high-octane**
> **thankfulness**

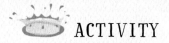 **ACTIVITY**

What's Your Metaphor?

 Which of the the metaphors described
in this chapter most clearly captures
your understanding of gratitude? Why?

 Write your own gratitude metaphor.

"The doors of happiness remain locked.
When they are unlocked,
they swing open quickly and widely
but close right behind them.
They must be reopened
throughout each day and there
is but one key that fits that lock:
Gratitude."

Fawn Weaver, author and founder
of HappyWivesClub.com

8
Lessons Learned

The end of "to-do"
list gratitude.

Receiving Grace

I used to think that growing in gratitude
required time and effort. I was convinced that
I needed to buy a special journal to record my
daily gratitudes, carve out a segment of time
to practise gratitude, and go on a retreat.

Each of these things required commitment and
perseverance, doing more, doing better, eliminating
all those things that were getting in the way. Yet
adding even one more thing to the to-do pile
resulted in gratitude becoming a burden rather than a
blessing. Gratitude should uplift us, not weigh us down.

I realized that growing in gratitude began with a
greater awareness of what I had, rather than did not
have, and living in that reality. I needed to turn my
mind to the ways in which I was supported by others.
I needed that second stone of gratitude (page 70).
I needed to become more receptive to the grace that
surrounded me, the benefits and blessings in my life
that I did absolutely nothing to merit or deserve.

 ## ACTIVITIES

Done, Not Do

Gratitude is rooted in what has been done, not on what you need to do. Replace your "to-do" list with a "been-done" list.

 Focus your attention for a moment on what other people have done for you in the past 24 hours. Try to resist the urge to focus on what you need to do for the next 24 hours.

It's Not About Us

Resist the urge to monitor your progress. Focusing on your gratitude performance will only undermine it. When you express thanks, you will be consumed by how your thanks is received and the reaction of the recipient.

 Instead of being self-absorbed, be absorbed by all the good that is being done for you by others.

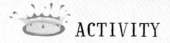 ## ACTIVITY

Give Yourself Grace

One of the biggest mistakes we can make is to think we should be grateful 100 per cent of the time. That's an impossible standard, so don't feel as though you've failed when you don't achieve it! We know gratitude is good for us, we know we should feel grateful, we know life would be better if we did, but sometimes the feeling is just not there and then we feel guilty about it.

◇ Take an inventory of all the good things you have done for other people. Celebrate your own strengths and admirable qualities.

Appreciate yourself

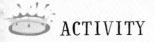

ACTIVITY

Lighting the Flame

"At times our own light goes out and is rekindled by a spark from another person. Each of us has cause to think with deep gratitude of those who have lighted the flame within us," wrote humanitarian Albert Schweitzer.

 Who has lit the flame in you? People who have helped us out of the darkness, out of hopelessness, who have found us when we have lost our way, and guided us back to the light. How can you show your gratitude to them now?

 **ACTIVITY**

Inspiration

Inspiration can be a powerful indicator that gratitude has transformed you in a significant way. Sometimes inspiration comes from witnessing acts of gratitude, more often it comes from our own experience of it.

 Are there ways in which feeling grateful has inspired you? What are they?

Thanksgiving

There are many
ways to show
gratitude and pass
along the goodness
we have received
from others.

When we give away the
goodness – a phrase I like
because it implies that we
express gratitude by using
our own gifts, talents, and
abilities instead of keeping them
to ourselves or otherwise squandering
them – gratitude becomes thanksgiving. The most
important lesson I have learned in my decade and
a half of studying gratitude is don't focus on yourself!
It's not until we realize this truth that we can truly
begin to reap the rewards of grateful living, and so
will those around us. Gratitude beckons.

Acknowledgements

A number of people have supported my dream to spread gratitude globally. I am especially grateful to Yvonne for her steadfast love and support. Doug Reid, Rick Cole, and Marc Afshar have been role models and constant sources of encouragement and inspiration. The Companywide Culture Committee at Southwest Airlines deserves a special shout-out for recognizing that gratefulness makes people great. Esmond Harmsworth, my agent extraordinaire, convinced me to move forward with this project, and my editor, Leanne Bryan, deserves my deep gratitude for her vision and for being amazingly easy to work with. A special thanks is due Kimon Sargeant for ensuring that the science of gratitude will continue to yield dividends for years to come.